PIANO SOLO

the twilight saga
breaking dawn
part 1

MUSIC FROM THE MOTION PICTURE SCORE
BY CARTER BURWELL

4 The Kingdom Where Nobody Dies

6 Cold Feet

9 What You See in the Mirror

12 Wedding Nightmare

14 Goodbyes

18 A Nova Vida

24 The Threshold

26 Honeymoon in Eclipse

32 Hearing the Baby

31 Let's Start with Forever

34 Hearts Failing

36 Bella Reborn

T0056526

ISBN 978-1-4584-2257-6

HAL•LEONARD®
CORPORATION

7777 W. BLUEMOUND RD. P.O. BOX 13819 MILWAUKEE, WI 53213

In Australia Contact:
Hal Leonard Australia Pty. Ltd.
4 Lentara Court
Cheltenham, Victoria, 3192 Australia
Email: ausadmin@halleonard.com.au

THE KINGDOM WHERE NOBODY DIES

Composed by
CARTER BURWELL

Very slowly

p

With pedal

Twice as fast

f

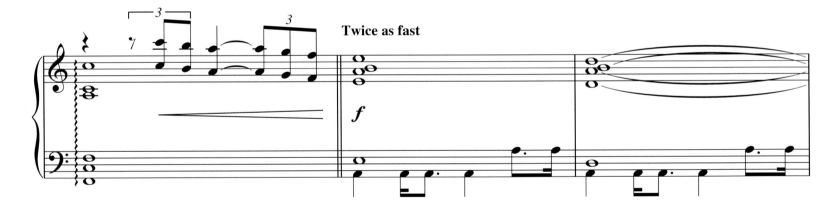

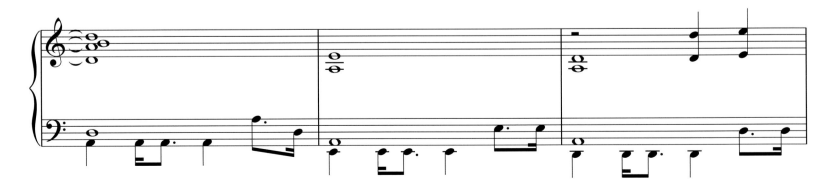

COLD FEET

Composed by
CARTER BURWELL

poco rit.

a tempo

WHAT YOU SEE IN THE MIRROR

Composed by
CARTER BURWELL

Segue to Wedding Nightmare

WEDDING NIGHTMARE

Composed by
CARTER BURWELL

Moderately slow

mp

With pedal

GOODBYES

Composed by
CARTER BURWELL

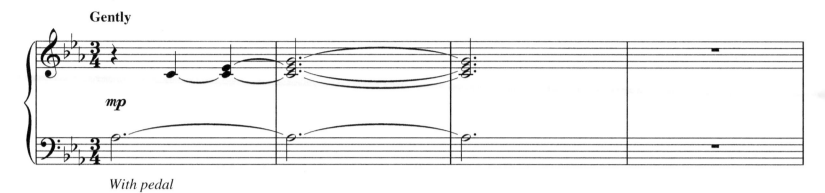

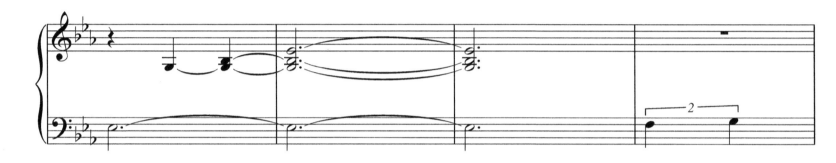

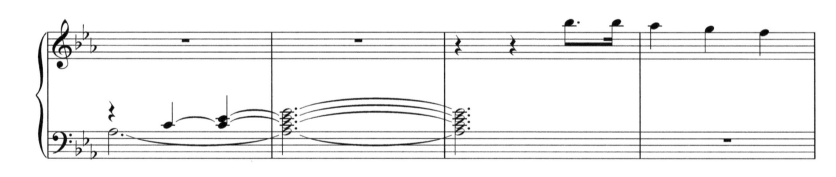

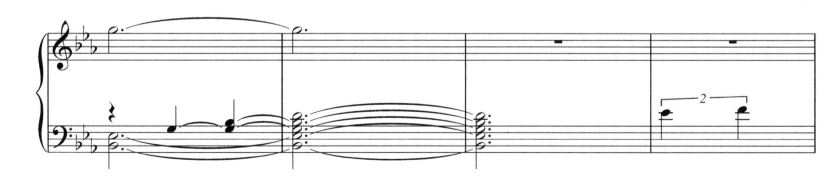

A NOVA VIDA

Composed by
CARTER BURWELL

Moderately

mp

With pedal

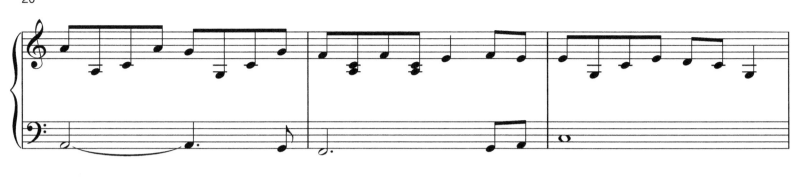

poco accel.

A little faster

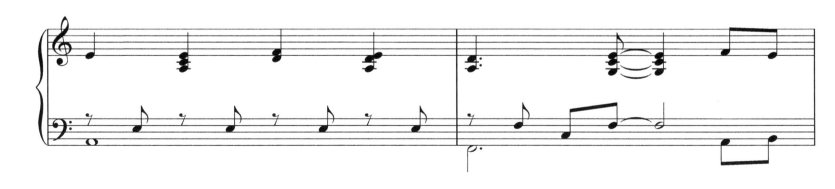

THE THRESHOLD

Composed by
CARTER BURWELL

HONEYMOON IN ECLIPSE

Composed by
CARTER BURWELL

With motion

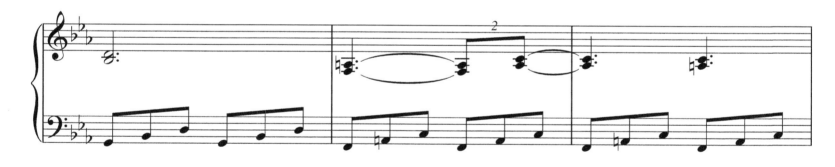

LET'S START WITH FOREVER

Composed by
CARTER BURWELL

HEARING THE BABY

Composed by
CARTER BURWELL

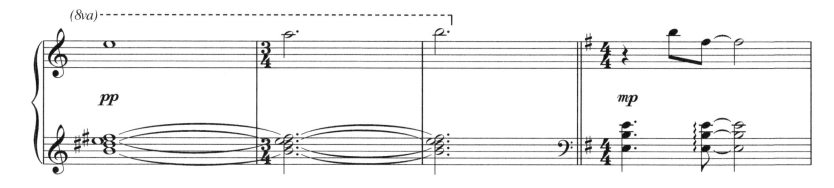

HEARTS FAILING

Composed by
CARTER BURWELL

BELLA REBORN

Composed by
CARTER BURWELL

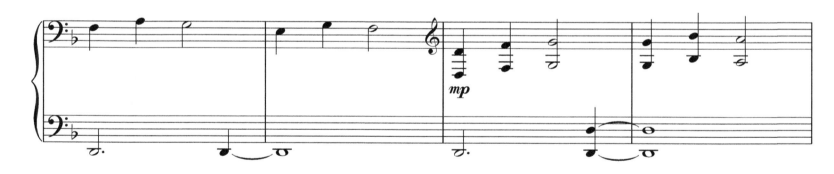